ECUMENICAL COUNCIL OF FIRST LYON

1245 AD

Innocent IV

Pope of Rome

Translated by: D.P. Curtin

ECUMENICAL COUNCIL OF FIRST LYON

Copyright @ 2021 Dalcassian Press

All rights reserved. No part of this publication may be reproduced, distributed, or transmitted in any form or by any means, including photocopying, recording, or other electronic or mechanical methods, without the prior written permission of the publisher, except in the case of brief quotations embodied in critical reviews and certain other non-commercial uses permitted by copyright law. For permission request, write to Dalcassian Press at dalcassianpublishing at gmail.com

ISBN: 979-8-3302-2478-4 (Paperback)

Library of Congress Control Number:
Author: Curtin, D.P. (1985-)

Printed by Ingram Content Group, 1 Ingram Blvd, La Vergne, Tennessee

First printing edition 2021.

COUNCIL OF LYON I
Ecumenical and General Council of the Catholic Church

Bishop Innocent, the servant of the servants of God, present at the holy council in eternal memory of the matter.

To the summit of the apostolic dignity, although assumed by the unworthy condescension of the divine majesty, we must exercise the care of all Christians diligently as a watchman, who must exercise skill and with the eye of intimate consideration to discern the merits of each one, and balance the balance of prudent deliberation, so that those whom just vigor has shown worthy of examination, we may raise with suitable favors, but those who are guilty with punishments let us weigh down, always weighing merit and reward in equal measure, recompense to each according to the quality of the work, the amount of punishment or grace.

Of course, since the terrible upheaval of the wars had long afflicted some provinces of the Christian profession, we desiring with all our affections the tranquility and peace of the holy church of God, and of the whole Christian people in general, to the principal secular prince, the agent of this dissension and tribulation, from the happy memory of Pope Gregory our predecessor for his excesses bound by the chain of anathema, special messengers, men of great authority, that is to say, the venerable brothers Peter of Alban, then archbishop of Rothomagens, and William of Sabine, then once of Mutinen, bishops and our beloved son William, cardinal priest of the basilica of the Twelve Apostles, then abbot of Saint Facundus, who were zealous for his safety .

And because the restoration of the prelates, the clerics, and all others whom he held captive, and all the clerics and laymen whom he had taken in helmets, could be the most inductive of peace, he was to restore them, both himself and his messengers, before they were called to the apostolate. we were to be obliged, they had promised, to be asked and asked of him, and we did it through them, and proposed, moreover, that they were ready for us to hear and negotiate peace, and also to hear the satisfaction which the prince wished to make of all those for whom he was bound by the bond of excommunication, and to be offered, moreover, that if the church had injured him in anything contrary to debt, which he did not believe, she was ready to correct him and to reform him into a state of debt.

And if he should say that he had in no way injured the church contrary to justice, or that we had injured him contrary to justice, we were ready to call the kings, prelates, and princes, both ecclesiastical and secular, to some safe place, where they could meet by themselves or solemn messages; by the counsel of the council, if he had injured him in anything, to make satisfaction for himself, and to recall the sentence, if he had unjustly brought it against him, and with all meekness and mercy, as far as was possible with God and his honor, to receive from the injuries and offenses of his own church which were inflicted by him you receive satisfaction from him.

The church also wished to keep all its friends who adhered to it in peace and to enjoy full security, so that they could never on this occasion suffer any crisis.

But even though we tried to insist with him on behalf of peace with fatherly admonitions and warnings with gentleness yet imitating the same harshness of Pharaoh and stopping his ears as an asp, he despised such prayers and warnings with obstinacy and obstinate exaltation.

And although the process of time on the day of the Lord's Supper was near and recently passed before us and our brothers, who were present in Christ our son, the illustrious emperor of Constantinople, a not small group of prelates, senators of the Roman people, and a great multitude of others, who on the same day because of the solemnity of his had assembled in different parts of the world to the apostolic see, that he would stand by our orders and that of the church, through the noble man Raymond, Count of Tholosan, and the magistrates Peter de Vinea and Tadeus de Suessa, the judges of his court, and his messengers and agents having a special command in this regard from him, took the oath; He did not fulfill what he had sworn.

On the contrary, it is probably believed that he performed it with that intention, as it is clearly gathered from the following facts, that he would mock the church and us rather than make amends, when a year and more had already passed, he could not be recalled to the church itself, nor did he take care to satisfy himself for the damages and injuries inflicted on him. although there was a requirement above this.

For this reason, unable to tolerate Christ's iniquities without a grievous offense, we are urgently compelled by conscience to take notice of the same.

And that for the present we may be silent about the rest of his crimes, he committed four very serious ones, which cannot be concealed by any dissimulation.

For he rejected many times; he has recklessly violated the peace once reformed between church and government; He also perpetrated a sacrilege, making prisoners of the cardinals of the holy Roman church and the prelates and clerics of other churches, religious and secular, coming to convene the council which the same predecessor had led. of heresy, too, he is regarded as suspect, not on doubtful and light grounds, but on difficult and evident grounds.

Indeed, it is quite clear that he committed several perjuries.

For once when he was staying in the parts of Sicily, before he had been elected to the dignity of empire, in the presence of Gregory of good memory, Saint Theodore, cardinal deacon, legate of the apostolic see, of happy memory to Pope Innocent, our predecessor, and to the successors of his church and of Rome, for the concession of the kingdom of Sicily made to him by the same church , he took the oath of fidelity and, as is said, the same, after he had been elected to the same position and came to the city, in the presence of the same Innocent as his brothers, and many others present, he renewed the law of humanity in his hands.

Then, when he was in Alamanni, he swore to the same Innocent and, when he had died, to Honorius, our predecessor and his successors, and to the Roman church itself, the present princes and nobles of the empire, to preserve and protect in good faith the honors, rights, and possessions of the Roman church as he could. and that whatever came into his hands, he would endeavor to restore without difficulty, the possessions expressly mentioned in this oath being named, which he afterwards confirmed, having already obtained the crown of the empire.

But there was a reckless violator of these three oaths, not without the mark of treason and the crime of injured majesty.

For against the aforesaid predecessor Gregory and his brethren, he presumed to send threatening letters to the same brethren, and the said Gregory to the brethren themselves, as appears from the letters addressed by him at that time to the same, and also, as is reported, to defame him in many ways throughout almost the whole world.

And he caused our venerable brother Otto of Portuenza, then cardinal deacon of St. Nicholas in the Tullian prison, and James of Praenestinus, bishops of good memory, legates of the apostolic see, noble and great members of the Roman church, to be personally arrested, and robbed of all their goods, and led more than once through different places to prisons with ignominy. to be freed

Moreover, the privilege which the Lord Jesus Christ delivered in him to the blessed Peter and his successors, namely: whatever you bind on earth shall be bound in heaven, and whatever you loose on earth shall be loosed in heaven, in which the authority and power of the Roman church certainly consists. He completely despised it, forcing others not to save it.

The possessions also of the aforesaid Roman church, viz. the Marchia, the Duchy, Benevento, whose walls and towers he destroyed, and others which he obtained in the parts of Tuscany and Lombardy and some other places, with a few exceptions, he does not fear to seize, and he still holds them occupied.

And as if it were not enough for him, that he came clearly contrary to the oaths that had been given, by presuming such things, he compelled by himself or his officials to reject the men of the same possessions, absolving them from the oaths of fidelity by which the Romans were bound to the church, by deed, when he could not by law, and making them do the same fidelity nevertheless to abjure the aforesaid that he would perform such oaths of fidelity.

But it is fully established that the violator of the peace himself exists, because when long ago, at the time of the peace between him and the reformed church, he had sworn before John of Abbat Villa of good memory, bishop of Sabine, and Master Thomasius, titular presbyter of Saint Sabina, in the presence of many prelates, princes, and barons, that he would stand and report precisely without any condition to all the commandments of the church upon those for whom he was bound by the bond of excommunication, the causes of the same excommunication expressed by order before him, then to all the Theotonics, men of the kingdom of Sicily, and any others who had adhered to the church against him, remitting all offense and punishment, and that at no time would he offend or cause them to be offended because of what they had stood for in the church, making an oath in his soul by Thomas, count of Acerra, afterwards peace and oaths of this kind, he did not keep in any way ashamed to be drawn into perjury.

For some of these men, as noble as others, he afterwards caused to be taken captive, and having robbed them of all their possessions, took their wives and children captive, and the lands of the church, contrary to the promise which he had made to John the Sabine bishop and Thomas the cardinal, he irreverently invaded, although they were then present to him. If he should offend, they promulgated the sentence of excommunication.

And when they had ordered the same to him by apostolic authority, that he should prevent neither by himself nor by another, that the demands, elections, and confirmations of the churches and monasteries in the aforesaid kingdom should be made freely of the rest, according to the statutes of the general council, and that no one thereafter in the same kingdom should ecclesiastical men and their affairs he would impose tallies or collects, that no cleric or ecclesiastical person there should be brought before a secular judge in any other civil or criminal case, unless the question of the fees was held civilly, and he would competently satisfy the Templars, Hospitallers and other ecclesiastical persons for the damages and injuries inflicted on them, himself He disdained to fulfill such a command.

For it is clear that eleven or more archbishoprics and many episcopal sees, also abbeys and other churches, are vacant at the present time in the aforesaid kingdom, those which, under the procurator himself, as is plainly evident, had long been abandoned by the rule of the prelates under the weight of their own prejudices and the danger of souls.

And although it may be that in some of the churches of the same kingdom elections were celebrated by the chapters, because the clerics of the same family were chosen by them, it may be concluded from a probable argument that they did not have the ability to choose freely.

And of the churches of his own kingdom, he not only caused the resources and goods to be seized as he wished, but also their crosses, torches, chalices, and other sacred treasures and silken cloths were taken away as a contemptuous act of divine worship, although, as is said, of the churches themselves, yet exacted first for them at a certain price, in they have been partly restored.

Indeed, the clergy are afflicted in many ways by gatherings and beatings, and are not only brought to the secular judgment, but as it is said they are forced to undergo duels, imprisoned, killed and tortured on gallows to the confusion and disgrace of the clerical order.

But the aforesaid Templars, Hospitallers, and ecclesiastical persons have not been compensated for the damages and injuries inflicted on them.

He, too, is certain to be the perpetrator of sacrilege. For when the aforesaid bishops of Porto and Praenestinum, and as many prelates of the churches and clerics, both religious and secular, had come to the apostolic seat for the celebration of the council which he himself had previously requested, they had been summoned by sea, the roads of the land being completely barred by his command, Ensius having the same destination with his son with a great number of helmets, and by other means a number of which had been seriously prepared long before in the maritime parts of Tuscia, having laid ambushes against them, in order that the preconceived virus might be more serious, he caused them to be taken by a sacrilegious venture, some of their own superiors and others drowned in this kind of capture, some also killed, and some put to flight by the pursuit of the enemy, and the rest were robbed of all their goods, and were brought from place to place into the kingdom of Sicily with contempt, and were there imprisoned in severe prisons.

Some of whom, drenched in wretchedness and oppressed by hunger, failed miserably.

Moreover, the suspicion of heretical perversity arose against him, when after the sentence of excommunication pronounced by the aforesaid John, bishop of Sabine, and Thomas the cardinal, and the said Pope Gregory tied him with the chain of anathema, and after the cardinals, prelates, and clerics of the Roman church, and others also at different times, to the see the apostolic seizure of those who came, he despised and despised the keys of the church, causing himself to be celebrated, or rather to profane what is divine in it, and he constantly asserted, as has been said above, that he did not fear the opinions of the aforesaid Pope Gregory.

Moreover, being bound by the detestable friendship of the Muslims, he sent messages and gifts several times to them, and received them in turn with honor and mirth from those whom the rite embraces, keeping them with them in his daily obsequies; whom, as it is seriously said, he had caused to be camped, he was not ashamed to depute guards.

And what is more execrable, once existing in the overseas parts, made by a kind of arrangement, or rather collusion with the sultan, allowed the name of Mahomet to be publicly proclaimed in the temple of the Lord day and night.

And lately the news of the sultan of Babylon, after the same sultan had inflicted on the holy land and the Christian inhabitants of it by himself and his people the most grievous damages and incalculable injuries, he caused the kingdom of Sicily with praises to the pride of the same sultan, as it is reported, to be received with honor and provided magnificently.

By abusing the pernicious and horrible obsequies of other infidels against the faithful, and those who, condemnably despising the apostolic see, departed from the unity of the church, endeavoring to join them by kinship and friendship, he made Louis of clear memory, duke of Bavaria, a special devotee of the Roman church, as it is assuredly asserted, despised the Christian religion by the murderers were slain, and Batatio, the enemy of God and the church, solemnly separated from the communion of the faithful by the sentence of excommunication, together with his helpers, counselors, and supporters, gave his daughter in marriage.

But rejecting the acts and manners of the Catholic princes, neglecting salvation and reputation, he does not focus on works of piety.

Nay, that we may be silent about his evil dissolutions, when he had learned to oppress, he did not care to relieve the oppressed mercifully, his hand, as befits a prince, was not extended to alms, when he insisted on the destruction of churches and afflicted the religious and other ecclesiastical persons with affliction; He is not seen to have built churches or monasteries or hospitals or other pious places.

Are not these, then, not light, but effective arguments for the suspicion of heresy against him? yet when he asserted that they were bound by the term of heretics by the civil law, and that they should succumb to the judgments passed against them, those who, even on the slightest argument, had been detected as deviating from the judgment of the Catholic religion and path.

In addition to these things, the kingdom of Sicily, which is the special patrimony of the blessed Peter and which the same prince held as a fief from the apostolic see, had already reduced the clergy and laity to such an emptying of servitude that they had almost nothing at all, and from then on almost all the righteous were driven out, those who remained there to live under the condition of a slave, and to offend the Roman Church, of which they are principally men and vassals, to offend in many ways and to attack hostilely.

He might also be justly criticized for having neglected to pay the annual pension of a thousand squifati, in which he is bound for the same kingdom of the Roman church itself, for nine years or more.

We, therefore, on the foregoing and as many other nefarious excesses of his, with our brethren and the sacred council, being careful to prevent them from deliberating, while the vices of Jesus Christ may be undeservedly held in our lands, as it was said in the person of the blessed Peter the apostle: Whatever you bind on earth and the rest, the aforesaid prince, who rendered himself so unworthy of government and kingdoms with all that honor and dignity, who, because of his iniquities, was rejected by God from reigning or commanding, bound by his sins and cast off from all the honor and dignity that we have shown him deprived of by the Lord, we denounce and nevertheless deprive by sentencing, all who are bound to him by an oath of fidelity, permanently absolved from such an oath, by firmly restraining the apostolic authority, that no one of the rest should pretend to be or intend to act as emperor or king, and by decreeing that anyone who afterwards gave him counsel, aid, or favor as emperor or king, subject to the bond of excommunication.

But those to whom the election of the emperor in the same government concerns, let them freely choose their successor.

ECUMENICAL COUNCIL OF FIRST LYON

We shall take care to provide for the aforesaid kingdom of Sicily with the advice of our brothers, as we see fit.

Give (then) to Lyons, 16th of the month of August, in the third year of our pontificate.

Since in many articles of law there are an infinite number of provisions, we decided that by a general clause certain others, which are frequently inserted in our letters, should not be brought into judgment beyond three or four.

The name of those in the first summons must be expressed by the petitioner so that there may be no room for fraud if he can freely vary about them.

By the present decree we have decided to provide that the cause should not be entrusted by the apostolic see or the legates to anyone except to persons who are either endowed with dignity or established in cathedral churches or other honorable collegiate bodies, and that such cases should not be conducted anywhere else than in states or large and distinguished places where it is worth having a legal supply of experts.

As for the judges who, contrary to this statute, have cited either party to other places, or both of them, shall not be punished with impunity, unless the citation proceeded by the common will of both parties.

Desiring to save the expense of equity lawsuits, by which we can laboriously curtail the statute of the happy memory of Pope Innocent the Third published above, we have decided that if anyone wishes to move several personal questions against another, he should seek to obtain letters on all such questions, not to different judges, but to the same.

But he who does the contrary shall be deprived of every advantage of the letters, and the process shall not be worth the habit through the same others, if he has exhausted him through them, he shall be condemned in legal expenses.

If, during the same trial, the accused has told the petitioner that he is liable to him by way of counterclaim or agreement, if he prefers to obtain a writ against him, he must be tried before the same judges, unless he can refuse them as suspects, and he will be punished by a similar punishment if he has committed a breach.

We decree that if anyone challenges the election demand or provision made in the form of objecting to something or a person and for this reason it happens to be appealed to us both the one who opposes and the one who defends and in general all those who are interested and whom the case happens to be in person or through agents appointed to the cause to the apostolic see from the day of the objection they should take the journey within a month.

But if any party does not come twenty days after the expected arrival of the other party, the business of the election shall, notwithstanding the absence of any one, be proceeded with according to law.

But we want and command that these should be observed in dignified persons and canons.

We also add that whoever does not fully prove that he objects in the form to the expenses that the other party has shown that he has incurred for this reason is condemned.

But he who fails in the proof of what he charges in person knows that he has been suspended from ecclesiastical benefices for three years.

And if within that time he has committed himself by his own recklessness, then he shall be permanently deprived of them by right, and he shall have no hope or confidence on this account of mercy, unless he has established by the most evident documents that he excuses himself from the fault of slander, a probable and sufficient cause.

In the elections and demands and scrutinies from which the right to choose arises, we completely reject alternative and uncertain conditional vows, decreeing that such vows instead of those taken from pure consent should celebrate the election by the voice of those who have not purely consented, falling back on others. We decide that the conservators whom we generally grant may defend against manifest injuries and violence those whom we entrust to them to defend, and that they may not extend their power to other things which require judicial inquiry.

It is the duty of our office to take care of the subjects by means of remedies, because while we shake off their burdens, while we remove the stumbling blocks, we rest in their tranquility and are sheltered in peace.

Therefore, by the present decree, we decree that the ambassadors of the Roman church, regardless of whether they have been sent by us or claim the dignity of their own churches under the pretext of the embassy, have no power to confer benefits from the office of the embassy, unless we have specifically directed this to be indulged in someone.

This, however, we do not want to be observed in our brothers acting as ambassadors, because just as they rejoice in the prerogative of honor, we want them to act with greater authority.

It does not seem to be ambiguous in law that a delegated judge who has not received a special command from the apostolic see to order that neither of the parties may appear before him in person in court unless the case is criminal or unless the necessity of the law demands that the parties be brought before him personally to tell the truth or by swearing an oath of slander.

The peremptory exception or the defense of any principal containing knowledge of the matter before the contested case is objected to unless the matter has been adjudicated or settled or ended.

A frequent and constant complaint surrounds us that the exception of spoliation, sometimes slanderously proposed in the courts, hinders and disturbs ecclesiastical causes.

For while the exception is insisted upon, appeals may be filed.

And so, the main knowledge of the cause is interrupted and generally destroyed.

And therefore, we who desire voluntary labors to prepare rest for others, desiring to put an end to lawsuits and to cut off the matter of slander, have decided that in civil cases the objection of spoliation proposed by someone other than the plaintiff will not postpone the judge's proceeding in the main.

But if in civil cases the plaintiff asserts that he has been robbed by the plaintiff, but in criminal cases the defendant asserts that he has been robbed of anything less than fifteen days after the date on which he is presented, he shall prove what he asserted, otherwise he shall be condemned for the expenses incurred by the plaintiff in the meantime by judicial assessment.

Others were to be punished if the judge saw fit.

But we want to understand him as robbed in this case, when he is criminally accused who asserts that he was robbed of all or the greater part of his substance by violence.

And to speak according to this, the canons must be believed with a sound understanding, because we must neither contend naked nor oppose unarmed enemies.

For he who has been robbed has the privilege of not being able to take off his clothes when he is already naked.

Now it is usual to doubt among the scholars whether the person who has been robbed by a third party can plead against his accuser, or whether he should be allowed time by the judge during which he implores restitution.

It may not be that he wishes to exist in such a way as to elude every accuser, which we consider quite consistent with equity.

And if he does not ask for restitution within the period of cancellation and does not bring the case to an end when he could, despite the exception of spoliation, he may be accused from now on.

To these things we decree that the spoliation of private property by an agent over the ecclesiastics is not to be applied at all.

A plaintiff who has caused the adversary to appear at the term for which he was summoned has not taken care of the coming of the defendant at the expense of this fact, is legally condemned to another summons unless he sufficiently takes care that his appearance at the term is at least not admissible.

We decree that he who disputes with another possessor over the dignity of his person or in obtaining an ecclesiastical benefice, because of the obstinacy of the adverse party, for the sake of keeping the thing in their possession, shall not be sent into their possession, lest by this entering into it he may be found guilty, but let it be permitted in this case to defy the divine absence by filling the presence, even if not disputed in the dispute, with care after examining the business itself to the end due to termination.

We have decided that the jury may admit negative positions which cannot be proved except by confession if they think it expedient in fairness.

With pious consideration, the mother church decreed that the exception of major excommunication in any part of the courts would delay the opposing suits and repel the agents, so that from this the ecclesiastical censure would be more feared and the danger of communion would be avoided. .

But with the increasing malice of men, what was provided for a remedy passes into harm.

For while in ecclesiastical cases this exception is more frequently opposed through malice, it happens that business is postponed and parties are exhausted by labor and expenses.

Therefore, since this disease has crept in as a common one, we thought it worthwhile to apply a common remedy.

If, therefore, a person opposes excommunication by his appearance and sets forth the name of the excommunicator, he shall be known to bring that matter into public notice, which he shall be able to prove by the most open documents within a period of eight days from the day on which it is proposed.

If the judge does not agree to proceed in the case, he will not leave the defendant in the expenses which the plaintiff has shown that he has incurred in those days, by condemning him with a preliminary assessment.

If, however, afterwards, during the trial and the sufficient amount of proof, the same or other excommunication is received again, and it is proved, the plaintiff shall be excluded in what follows, until he deserves to obtain the grace of absolution, the foregoing will nevertheless remain in force.

Provided that this exception shall not be proposed more than two times, unless a new excommunication has arisen, or there has been clear and prompt proof of an old one. But if such an exception is proposed after the matter has been decided, it will prevent the execution, but the sentence that preceded it will have no less force, provided that if the plaintiff has been publicly excommunicated and the judge knows this at any time, even if the defendant does not object to this, the judge will not postpone the removal of the plaintiff from his office.

Since the tribunal of the eternal prince does not have that guilty person whom the judge unjustly condemns on the testimony of the prophet, nor will he condemn him when he is judged.

But they carry the balance in their hands and weigh the spears with equal balance, so that in all that is to be done in cases, especially in conceiving and delivering judgments, they keep in mind only the god, imitating the example of him who entered the tabernacle and reported the complaints of the people to the master to judge according to his command.

But if any ordinary ecclesiastical judge or delegate, prodigal of fame and a persecutor of his own honor, against conscience and against justice, does anything in court to the detriment of another party, through grace or through dirt, he knows that he is suspended from the execution of his office for a year from the execution of his office, and knows that he is suspended for the assessment of the suit against the party he has injured, nevertheless he will be known to be condemned because if, during the suspension, he condemnably engages himself in the trap of divine irregularity, he will wrap himself in the trap of divine irregularity, according to canonical sanctions, from which he can only be freed by the apostolic see, save by other constitutions which carry and inflict punishments on judges who make bad judgments.

Indeed, it is worthy that he who presumes to offend in so many ways should be punished with multiple punishments.

It is our heart to reduce the disputes and to relieve the subjects from their labors.

We decree, therefore, that if any person, in court or outside of interlocutory proceedings, or of grievance, brings to us an appeal to assign the cause of appeal in writing, he shall forward it to the apostles whom we command to be presented to him.

In which the judge shall express the cause of the appeal and why the appeal was not admitted, or if the appeal was brought perhaps out of respect for the superior.

After this, according to the geographical distance of the persons and the quality of the matter, I will cancel the prosecution at the time of the prosecution, if the appellant wishes, and if the principals have requested by themselves or through their agents, instructed to act with reasons and defenses relating to the case, they should approach the apostolic see so prepared that, if it seems to us, to expedite the finished article of the appeal or, subject to the will of the parties, he shall proceed in the main business as far as he can and must by law, without changing what antiquity has established in appeals from definitive sentences.

If the appellant does not comply with the foregoing, he shall be deemed not to have appealed, and the examination shall return to the previous judge to be ordered to pay legal expenses.

If, however, the appellant has disobeyed this statute, he shall be proceeded against as a recalcitrant, both in costs and in cause, as far as is permitted by law.

ECUMENICAL COUNCIL OF FIRST LYON

It is indeed just that the rights should rise against him who eludes the right judge and the party.

When a legitimate cause of suspicion is assigned against a judge, and arbitrators chosen by the parties according to the form of the law, who know about it, it often happens that those who do not want to agree to the same and do not plead a third party with which both or one of them proceed to the decision of the matter itself, so that the judge is bound to pronounce a sentence of excommunication against those who themselves both because of hatred and because of favor they despised longer.

Wherefore the case itself, being prolonged further, does not proceed to the knowledge of the principal business.

Therefore, wishing to apply a necessary remedy to this disease, we decided that the arbitrators themselves, through the judge, should fix a proper limit below which they agree on the same thing, or that they summon a third party in agreement with whom both or one of them will try to terminate the business of the same suspicion.

Otherwise, the judge will not fail to proceed in the main business from then on.

For the redemption of the human race, descending from the highest heavens to the bottom of the world, and finally undergoing a temporary death, the son of God, Jesus Christ, lest after the resurrection he ascend the flock redeemed by his own glorious blood to the father without a shepherd, he would abandon his care to the blessed Peter the apostle, that by his steadfastness of faith he might strengthen the rest of them in the Christian religion which he undertook to inflame minds with the ardor of devotion to the works of his salvation.

Wherefore we, who are the undeserved successors of the same apostle's disposition to the lord, may be the undeserved successors of his redeemer on the earth, though unworthily holding the place of the same redeemer in the world, and being concerned about the care of the same flocks, we must be awakened by vigilance with concern for the care of the same flocks, and we must concentrate on the salvation of the yoke of the yoke of thought, suppressing the harmful and acting beneficially, so as to shake off from us the sleep of our negligence, and care in the eyes of the heart. let us be able, by diligent watchfulness, to win the very souls to God by his grace cooperating with us.

When, then, those who, with such horrible inhumanity and cruelty, thirst for the death of others, that they may themselves be killed by murderers, not only seek the death of bodies, but also of souls, unless the exuberant divine grace precedes them, that they may be protected by spiritual weapons, and that all power be given by the Lord to exercise right justice and judgment we are willing to meet with such a danger of souls and to strike such evil presumptuous ecclesiastical with the beak of notice that the fear of punishment is the goal of this presumption, especially since some magnates, fearing such extremes, have been forced to obtain security from the master of their murderers, so that.

From him, not without dishonor to Christian dignity, we decided to redeem his life in a certain way, with the approval of the holy council, so that whoever the prelate prince or any other ecclesiastical or secular person caused or even ordered to kill any of the Christians by the aforesaid assassins, although death may not follow from this, or received or defended or concealed them The sentences of excommunication and deposition from dignity, honor, order, duty, and beneficence incur automatically, and these may be freely communicated to others by those to whom their contribution belongs.

Even with all his worldly goods, as a rival of the Christian religion, let him be perpetually distrusted by the whole Christian people, and after it has been established by probable documents that he has committed some crime so heinous, no other sentence of excommunication, deposition, or distrust is required against him.

Since excommunication is curative, not mortal, disciplining, not eradicating, so long as it does not despise the person to whom it was sent, let the ecclesiastical judge carefully see to it that what is carried out in it shows that he is pursuing what is correcting and healing.

Whoever, therefore, excommunicates himself, must state in writing, and express the cause for which he is excommunicated.

But the excommunicated person is bound to hand over a copy of this writing within a month after the day of the sentence, if requested.

Upon which request we wish to be made a public instrument or certified letters sealed with an authentic seal.

But if any judge who violates this kind of constitution recklessly exists for one month from entering the church and knowing that he is suspended.

On the other hand, the superior to whom the appeal is made, relaxing the sentence itself without difficulty, condemns the excommunicating party to the costs and all that is involved, or punishes others with a commensurate remark, so that the judges learn how serious it is to strike sentences of excommunication without due maturity.

And these same things we want to observe in the sentences of suspension and prohibition.

Let the prelates of the churches and the judges of the whole world be careful not to incur the aforesaid penalty of suspension.

And if it happens that they continue the divine offices as before, they do not escape irregularity according to the canonical sanctions which can only be dispensed with by the supreme pontiff. It is usually called into question by some whether when a person asks for absolution by a superior as a precaution, while he asserts that the sentence of excommunication extended to him is no obstacle without contradiction, the duty of absolution should be paid to him, and whether before such absolution he who offers himself in court will prove himself bound by a legitimate excommunication after an appeal, or that there was an intolerable error in the sentence should be clearly expressed in the rest except that article of proof to be avoided.

Therefore, in the first doubt, we decide to observe that the acquittal of the petitioner is not denied, even if the excommunicator or the adversary opposes himself in this, unless he says that he was excommunicated for a clear offense, in which case a term of eight days will be granted to him who says so.

So that if he has proved what he opposes, the sentence will not be relaxed unless a sufficient remedy is first provided, or a competent warning of reparation if a doubtful offense is proposed.

In the second question, we decide that the one who is admitted to the trial pending the trial article in the rest of what he has accepted as a plaintiff in the courts is meanwhile avoided outside the court but is nevertheless admitted in requests and elections and other legal acts.

We have decreed that no judge may presume to excommunicate those who have been excommunicated by him in speech and others to whom he is bound by a minor excommunication before a canonical admonition to excommunicate the greater, save the constitutions lawfully promulgated against those who are condemned to participate in the crime.

But if, by the expression and other things by which the participant slips into a minor excommunication, the judge may, after a canonical reminder, condemn such participants to a similar censure.

ECUMENICAL COUNCIL OF FIRST LYON

Otherwise, the excommunication pronounced on the participants will not hold, and those who pronounce it will be able to fear a legitimate punishment.

Because it is dangerous for the bishops and their superiors, on account of the execution of the pontifical office, which frequently falls upon them, that in any case of interdict or suspension they incur the sentence automatically, we have decided, provided by deliberation, that the bishops and other superior prelates of no constitution, on the occasion of the sentence or mandate, shall in no way incur the aforesaid sentence except in the bishops and their superiors themselves are expressly mentioned.

We also add to this sanction that what is usually established in the constitution by some of us until now has been established that when someone offers himself to be tried in court after a legitimate appeal of excommunication he is bound by the sentence pending the article of proof in those things that are dealt with outside the court by elections demands offices and other legitimate acts not It should be avoided that the decisions of bishops and archbishops should not be extended in any way, but that it should obtain in the future what was once observed in such acts.

Pastoral concern worries us and urges us to counsel fallen churches and to ensure that they do not fall in the future with a healthy constitution.

When, therefore, the storm of usury has almost destroyed many churches, and some of the prelates are found to be very negligent about the payment of debts, especially those contracted by their predecessors, and to be remiss, and to incur greater debts and to oblige the things of the church, they are too lazy to keep the things they have found, preferring to do a little for their own praise rather than good. to preserve the dismissed recover the lost restore and repair the ruins we do not excuse ourselves from the rest for a less useful administration and pour their guilt on our predecessors or others, we sanction with the approval of the present council that the rest of the pontiffs, abbots, and deans who carry out a legitimate and common administration within one month after they have approached the administration as previously intimated next superior as per se.

Or, through some suitable and faithful ecclesiastical person, it may be interposed by those present that the chapter or meeting specially summoned for this purpose should draw up an inventory of the things taken up by the administration, in which movable and immovable books, paper, instruments, privileges, ornaments, or ecclesiastical vestments, and everything that pertains to the instruction of the urban or rural estate, as well as the debts and Credibles must be carefully recorded so that in what state they have taken over the church or administration and governed it in the course of time, and in the event of death or resignation they have dismissed by the superior if necessary and those who are assigned to the services of the churches are clearly known.

As for the archbishops who, besides the superior Roman pontiff, do not have any of the suffragans either personally or through another, as has been expressed above, and the abbots and other minor prelates exempt one neighboring bishop who claims no right for himself in the exempt church, they should endeavor to summon for this purpose the inventory of both the substituted prelates and of his collegium as well as of the superior suffragans or neighboring bishops of those called for this purpose shall be protected by seals in the archives of the church with due caution and nevertheless the transcript of the same inventory both the same institute and the prelate called for this purpose shall be similarly sealed.

Also, the funds are to be kept faithfully, and a worthy administration is given to them, and the debts found on the movables of the church are, if possible, to be paid with speed.

If, however, the movables are not sufficient to make a speedy payment, all the proceeds shall be converted into the payment of the debts which have been usurious or even burdensome, deducting from the proceeds themselves the necessary expenses, which are reasonably calculated by the presiding college.

But if the debts are not burdensome or usurious, a third part of the same proceeds, or a greater one, with the advice of those whom we have said to be called to make the inventory, shall be deputed for such satisfaction.

Furthermore, by the authority of the same council, we firmly prevent the aforesaid from obliging their persons or the churches entrusted to them on behalf of others, nor from contracting debts on behalf of themselves or the churches themselves, which may threaten to be burdensome.

If, however, an obvious necessity urges, or the reasonable expediency of the churches suggests, the prelate, with the superior archbishops and abbots, exempted from the aforesaid colleges, that by the council and consent of their own, the debts are not usurious, if possible, never contract in the fairs or public markets; the debt, even if it is for the benefit of the church, and we do not want ecclesiastical persons or churches to be bound to it in any way.

Indeed, the privileges of the churches, which we command to be kept faithfully in a safe place, are by no means bound to be pledged, nor are other things, except perhaps for necessary and useful debts contracted with the aforesaid solemnity.

But in order that this wholesome constitution may be inviolably observed, and that the fruits which we hope may result from it may appear, we have decided to order, and irrevocably decree, that all abbots and priors, as well as deans or superiors of cathedrals or other churches, at least once a year in their own collegiums, in the district of their administration, make an account of their administration, and before the visiting superior written and consigned, this account will be faithfully recited.

The archbishops and bishops, however, should try with due fidelity to convey the state of the administration of the goods belonging to their own table in the same way every year to their chapters, and nevertheless to the metropolitan bishops and metropolitan delegates of the apostolic see or to others to whom the visitation of their churches has been delegated by the same see.

But the written calculations shall always be reserved in the treasury of the church for memory, so that in the calculation of the following years of the past and the present, a careful comparison may be made, from which the superior administrator may comprehend the carelessness or negligence, which indeed negligence, having only God before the eyes of man, put aside by love, hatred or fear, will be punished by such and such an observation that He deserves neither from God nor from his superior or the apostolic see to receive vengeance for this.

And not only from future prelates, but also from those who have already been promoted, we command that the present constitution be observed.

Our arduous mind, occupied with the affairs of our care, which, distracted by various other matters of attention, watches over with an eye to the liberation of the empire of Constantinople. For a long time, the Catholics did not struggle without heavy labors and burdensome costs, with sweats and shedding of blood, nor was the government itself able to be completely rescued from the yoke of the enemies by the hindering sins, because of which we are troubled with not undeserved pain.

However, since the body of the church, for the sake of a dear member, that is to say, lacking the aforesaid government, would incur the mark of disgraceful deformity, and would suffer a painful loss of infirmities, which might be imputed to our worth and the negligence of the church itself, if the faithful were deprived of the vote and left to the enemies to be freely oppressed, we propose with a firm intention to assist the same government with effective and speedy relief, so that the church rising up to him for succor, that by reaching out the fortified government itself might be able to be rescued from the dominion of its adversaries, and that the master might feel the unity of the same body brought back by the master, that after the crushing hammer of the enemies, the consoling right hand of the mother of the church, and after the blindness of erroneous assertion, he might resume the sight of the Catholic faith.

But for the liberation of the same, the prelates of the churches, other than ecclesiastical men, are bound to exist with vigilance and intent, and to offer the help and labor that is necessary to further the increase of the same faith and ecclesiastical freedom, which would principally result from such a liberation.

Mainly because while the aforesaid government is aided, consequently aid is expended on the holy land.

Of course, in order that the aforesaid government may have a speedy and useful grant, we have decreed, with the general approval of the council, that half of all the proceeds of dignities and personages, as well as ecclesiastical supplies, other than ecclesiastical benefices, to those persons who do not make a personal residence in them for six months at least, whether they have one or more, to those who to ours and to our brothers and to their superiors, they stay in obedience, or they are on a pilgrimage, or they manage the affairs of their schools or churches by their command, or they assume or assume the sign of the cross in the aforesaid lands, or they go in person in the same government unless they have recourse, and if.

Some of the same except those who were crucified and proceeding from ecclesiastical revenues exceeding the value of one hundred marks of silver receive annually a third part of the remainder of the empire to be collected in relief by those who have been ordained for this purpose by apostolic providence until they are fully deputed for three years, notwithstanding any customs or statutes of the churches or any indulgences themselves. to churches or to persons granted by the apostolic see with an oath or strengthened by any other firmness.

And if, by chance, they have knowingly committed fraud on top of this, they incur the sentence of excommunication. We, however, from the findings of the Roman church, having previously been deputed from them as a tenth of the land deputed, will give the aforesaid tenth for the aforesaid subsidization of the empire in full.

Moreover, when the same government is aided, aid is provided most powerfully to the land itself, and to its recovery it is especially insisted on, while the government labors for its liberation, through the mercy of Almighty God and the blessed apostles Peter and Paul. let us indulge ourselves in that pardon of our sins, that by that privilege we may enjoy the immunity which we wish to be granted to the inhabitants of the aforesaid land.

It is known that the whole of the children of the church, not only innumerable expenses, but an inestimable affluence of blood, have poured out, as we gather from that sorrowful heart, what happened a long time ago against the faithful who fought against the ungodly in overseas parts.

But since it is for this reason that it is the wish of the apostolic see above all that the common desire for the redemption of the land may quickly come to God's propitiation, we have provided a worthy completion in order to encourage you by our letters to procure God's favor in business.

Therefore we beseech you all and beseech you in the name of the Lord Jesus Christ to the extent that each one of you is faithful to the people committed to your care in your preachings or when you have commanded them to repent by the pious admonitions granted upon this as you see fit a special indulgence as in the testaments that for a time have done something in the holy land or the government of Romania will leave a subsidy for the forgiveness of their sins to be provided more carefully so that what they have given in respect to the crucifixion in money for this subsidy may be kept faithfully in certain places under your seals and those that have been bequeathed for this purpose in other matters should be carefully reduced in writing.

And this work of piety, in which the cause of God alone is sought, and the salvation of the faithful is procured, so that your sincerity may be pursued with prompt affections, that at last you may safely await the reward of heavenly glory from the hand of the heavenly judge.

Desiring the worship of the Christian religion to be spread far and wide over all the world, we shall be pierced with a weapon of inestimable pain, if ever some people in this part meet with a desire contrary to ours, and with the effect that they endeavor to wipe the very worship completely from the face of the earth with all their earnestness and all their power.

Of course, the impious nation of the Tartars, desiring to subjugate the Christian people, or rather to exterminate them, having gathered some time ago with the forces of their nations, entered Poland, Russia, Hungary, other countries than the Christians, and made such a depopulating rage on them that with his sword he did not spare age or sex, but indiscriminately unleashed upon them all with horrible cruelty and unheard of extermination. and the kingdoms of others, with continued progress, she subdues to her own incessant persecution with the same idle sword in its scabbard, so that subsequently, invading the stronger Christian armies in strength, she may exercise her cruelty more fully upon them, so that in the darkness that is absent from the faithful, the faith of the world is exasperated, while the worshipers of her own nation, taken away from her, groan with the ferocity of her people.

Therefore, lest the intention of the same nation should succeed in such a detestable manner, but rather fail by God's authority, and on the contrary be concluded with an event attended to by all Christians, it must be weighed with consideration and procured with diligent effort, so that this process may be hindered in such a way that it cannot pass to them any further by the armed arm of the mighty.

For this reason, by a sacred and persuasive council, we admonish and exhort you all, carefully commanding the extent of the way and approach by which the nation itself could enter into our land, searching them very skillfully with ditches and walls or other buildings or artifices, as you see fit, to take care to guard in such a way that the entrance of the same nation to you is open from it cannot be easy.

But before the arrival of the apostolic see can be announced, so that you may be able to help the Lord by designating it as a refuge for you faithful against the attempts and attacks of the nation itself.

For we will contribute generously to the necessary and useful expenses which you have incurred for this purpose, and we will contribute proportionately from all the Christian countries when the common dangers are met with by this, and nevertheless we intend letters similar to the present to these other Christians through whose parts the aforesaid nation might have access.

Afflicted in heart for deploring the perils of the holy land, but especially for those established in it, the faithful know that it has happened anew to deliver God's mercy from the hands of the ungodly. All those who have decided to cross should meet in places suitable for this purpose.

Of whom they should proceed in the support of the same land with the divine and apostolic blessing.

But the priests and other clerics who have been in the Christian army, both subordinates and superiors, insist diligently on prayer and exhortation, teaching them by word as well as by example, so that they may always have the fear and love of the Lord before their eyes, lest they say or do anything that offends the majesty of the eternal king.

And if at any time they have fallen into sin through true repentance, let them soon rise again, wearing humility of heart and body, and maintaining moderation both in diet and in clothing, completely avoiding dissensions and rivalries, completely relegating themselves to rancor and bitterness, so that, armed with spiritual and material weapons, they can fight more securely against the enemies of the faith. not presuming on their own power but hoping on divine power.

Indeed, the noble and powerful armies, and all those abounding in riches, should be led by the admonitions of the pious superiors, that in view of the crucifix for which they took the sign of the cross, they should abstain from useless and superfluous expenses, but especially from those which are made in gatherings and banquets, and exchange them for the support of those persons through whom the business of God is worth prospering and For this reason, according to the providence of their superiors, forgiveness of their sins should be granted.

And we grant the aforesaid clerics that they may receive their benefices in full for three years, and that they should be resident in the churches, and, if necessary, that they may be able to pledge them during the same period.

Therefore, lest this holy purpose should be hindered or retarded, we command all the prelates of the churches to recall in their own places those who have laid down the sign of the cross, and to warn and induce them more diligently to return their vows to the Lord, as well as others who have been crucified and who happen to be still signed, and if necessary by they address the sentences of excommunication in person and the ban on their lands, ceasing all backbiting.

For these things, that nothing should be omitted in the business of Jesus Christ concerning the contingent, we desire and command that the patriarchs, archbishops, bishops, abbots, and others who have the care of souls should earnestly propose to the people committed to them the word of the cross, beseeching through the father and the son and the holy spirit, the only true eternal God, kings, leaders, princes, marquises, and counts. and the barons, other than the magnates, as well as the common states of the towns and cities, so that those who have not personally come to the support of the holy land should contribute a competent number of warriors with the necessary expenses for three years, according to their own resources, for the remission of their sins, as was expressed in the general letters which we sent long ago throughout the world, and to A greater caution will also be expressed below.

For we wish to be partakers of this release, not only those who will present their own ships for this purpose, but also those who are interested in building ships for this purpose.

But to those who refuse, if they have perhaps been so ungrateful to our Lord God, let us firmly protest on the apostolic side, that they may know that they will answer for this before a terrible judge on the last day of the district examination. into the hands of the father, if they refuse to serve him crucified for sinners in this matter, as if they were properly their own.

Moreover, by the general approval of the council, we decreed that all clerics, both subordinates and prelates, should contribute the whole twentieth part of the proceeds of the churches up to a period of three years to the support of the holy land by the hands of those who have been ordained for this purpose by apostolic providence, with the exception of certain religious excepting from this payment by merit exempting those who similarly assumed or assuming the sign of the cross they are going to go personally.

Let us and our brothers, the cardinals of the holy Roman church, pay the tithe in full, let them know that they are all bound to observe this faithfully by the sentence of excommunication, so that those who knowingly commit fraud on this account incur the sentence of excommunication.

Of course, because by the just judgment of the heavenly emperor's submission to the obedience of the heavenly emperor, the special prerogative should be enjoyed by the crucified, that they should be free from any other burdens than those collected or tallied. to the protectors being specially deputed for this purpose, so that until their return or death is most certainly known, they may remain whole and quiet, and if anyone presumes against them, they may be checked by ecclesiastical censures.

But if those who go thither to pay usury are bound by an oath, their creditors are obliged to remit the oath they have given them, and to desist from the exaction of usury, we order them to be compelled by the same distraint.

But if any of the creditors has compelled them to pay usury, we command them to restore them with a similar forced notice.

But we order the Jews to be compelled by secular power to remit usury, and until they have remitted them, they shall be denied communion altogether by the sentence of excommunication from all the faithful.

For those who are unable to pay their debts to the Jews at present, let the secular leaders provide a useful delay, so that after the journey has been taken, until their return or death is known, the inconvenience of interest does not fall upon the Jews, who are forced to count the proceeds of the pledges which they themselves have received in the meantime, after deducting the necessary expenses, since this kind of benefit does not seem to have much. an expense which prolongs the payment so as not to absorb the debt.

Moreover, let the prelates of the churches who have been negligent in rendering justice to the crucified and their families know that they will be severely punished.

LATIN TEXT

Concilium Lugdunense I

Concilia oecumenica et generalia Ecclesiae catholicae

Innocentius episcopus servus servorum Dei sacro praesente concilio ad rei memoriam sempiternam.

Ad apostolicae dignitatis apicem licet indigni dignatione divinae maiestatis assumpti, omnium christianorum curam vigili sedula que solertia gerere ac intimae considerationis oculo singulorum discernere merita et providae deliberationis statera librare debemus, ut quos iusti vigor examinis dignos ostenderit, congruis attollamus favoribus, quos autem reos poenis debitis deprimamus, appendentes semper meritum et praemium aequa lance, retribuendo cuique iuxta qualitatem operis, poenae vel gratiae quantitatem.

Sane cum dira guerrarum commotio nonnullas professionis christianae provincias diutius afflixisset, nos toto cupientes mentis affectu tranquillitatem et pacem ecclesiae sanctae Dei ac generaliter cuncto populo christiano, ad praecipuum principem saecularem, huiusmodi dissensionis et tribulationis actorem, a felicis recordationis Gregorio papa praedecessore nostro pro suis excessibus anathematis vinculo innodatum, speciales nuntios, magnae auctoritatis viros, videlicet venerabiles fratres Petrum Albanensem, tunc Rothomagensem archiepiscopum, et Guillelmum Sabinensem, tunc quondam Mutinensem, episcopos ac dilectum filium nostrum Guillelmum basilicae Duodecim apostolorum presbyterum cardinalem, tunc abbatem sancti Facundi, qui salutem zelabantur ipsius, duximus destinandos, facientes sibi proponi per ipsos, quod nos et fratres nostri quantum in nobis erat pacem per omnia se cum habere necnon cum omnibus hominibus optabamus, parati sibi pacem et tranquillitatem dare ac mundo etiam universo.

Et quia praelatorum, clericorum omnium que aliorum, quos detinebat captivos, et omnium tam clericorum quam laicorum, quos coeperat in galeis, restitutio poterat esse pacis plurimum inductiva, eum ut illos restitueret, cum hoc idem tam ipse quam sui nuntii, antequam ad apostolatus vocati essemus officium, promisissent, rogari et peti ab ipso fecimus per eosdem ac proponi insuper, quod iidem parati pro nobis erant audire et tractare pacem ac etiam audire satisfactionem, quam facere vellet princeps de omnibus, pro quibus vinculo erat excommunicationis astrictus, et offerri praeterea, quod si ecclesia eum in aliquo contra debitum laeserat, quod non credebat, parata erat corrigere ac in statum debitum reformare.

Et si diceret ipse, quod in nullo contra iustitiam laeserat ecclesiam vel quod nos eum contra iustitiam laesissemus, parati eramus vocare reges, praelatos et principes tam ecclesiasticos quam saeculares ad aliquem tutum locum, ubi per se vel solemnes nuntios convenirent, erat que parata ecclesia de consilio concilii sibi satisfacere, si eum laesisset in aliquo, ac revocare sententiam, si quam contra ipsum iniuste tulisset, et cum omni mansuetudine ac misericordia, quantum cum Deo et honore suo fieri poterat, recipere de iniuriis et offensis ipsi ecclesiae suis que per eum irrogatis gatis satisfactionem ab ipso.

Volebat etiam ecclesia omnes amicos suos sibi que adhaerentes in pace ponere plena que securitate gaudere, ut numquam hac occasione possent aliquod subire discrimen.

Sed licet sic apud eum pro pace paternis monitis et precum insistere curaverimus lenitate, idem tamen Pharaonis imitatus duritiam et obturans more aspidis aures suas, huiusmodi preces et monita elata obstinatione ac obstinata elatione despexit.

Et licet processu temporis in die coenae Domini proximo nuper praeterita praecedente coram nobis et fratribus nostris, praesentibus carissimo in Christo filio nostro Constantinopolitano imperatore illustri, coetu quoque non modico praelatorum, senatoribus populo que Romano et maxima multitudine aliorum, qui eodem die propter solemnitatem ipsius de diversis mundi partibus ad apostolicam sedem convenerant, quod staret nostris et ecclesiae mandatis per nobilem virum Raymundum comitem Tholosanum ac magistros Petrum de Vinea et Tadeum de Suessa curiae suae iudices, nuntios et procuratores suos speciale super hoc ab ipso mandatum habentes, praestiterit iuramentum, postmodum tamen quod iuraverat non implevit.

Quin immo ea intentione ipsum praestitisse probabiliter creditur, sicut ex factis sequentibus colligitur evidenter, ut eidem ecclesiae ac nobis illuderet potius quam pareret, cum anno et amplius iam elapso nec ad ipsius ecclesiae graemium revocari potuerit nec sibi de illatis ei damnis et iniuriis curaverit satisfacere, licet super hoc exstiterit requisitus.

Propter quod non valentes absque gravi Christi offensa eius iniquitates amplius tolerare, cogimur urgente nos conscientia iuste animadvertere in eundem.

Et ut ad praesens de ceteris eius sceleribus taceamus, quatuor gravissima, quae nulla possunt celari tergiversatione, commisit.

Deieravit enim multotiens; pacem quondam inter ecclesiam et imperium reformatam temere violavit; perpetravit etiam sacrilegium, capi faciens cardinales sanctae Romanae ecclesiae ac aliarum ecclesiarum praelatos et clericos, religiosos et saeculares, venientes ad concilium quod idem praedecessor duxerat convocandum; de haeresi quoque non dubiis et levibus sed difficilibus et evidentibus argumentis suspectus habetur.

Plura siquidem eum commisisse periuria satis patet.

Nam olim cum in Siciliae partibus morabatur, priusquam esset ad imperii dignitatem electus, coram bonae memoriae Gregorium sancti Theodori diacono cardinali, apostolicae sedis legato, felicis recordationis Innocentio papae praedecessori nostro et successoribus eius ecclesiae que Romanae, pro concessione regni Siciliae ab eadem ecclesia sibi facta, fidelitatis praestitit iuramentum et, sicut dicitur, illud idem, postquam ad eandem dignitatem electus exstitit et venit ad Urbem, coram eodem Innocentio suis que fratribus, aliis multis praesentibus, ligium hominium in eius faciens manibus, innovavit.

Deinde cum in Alamannia esset, eidem Innocentio et, ipso defuncto, bonae memoriae Honorio papae praedecessori nostro et eius successoribus ac ipsi ecclesiae Romanae, praesentibus imperii principibus atque nobilibus, iuravit honores, iura et possessiones Romanae ecclesiae pro posse suo servare ac protegere bona fide, et quod quaecumque ad manus suas devenirent, sine difficultate restituere procuraret, nominatis expresse dictis possessionibus in huiusmodi iuramento; quod postmodum confirmavit, coronam imperii iam adeptus.

Sed horum trium iuramentorum temerarius exstitit violator non sine proditionis nota et laesae crimine maiestatis.

Nam contra praefatum praedecessorem Gregorium et fratres suos comminatorias litteras eisdem fratribus destinare ac dictum Gregorium apud fratres ipsos, sicut apparet per litteras ab eo tunc directas eisdem, et etiam, prout fertur, per universum fere orbem terrarum multipliciter diffamare praesumpsit.

Ac venerabilem fratrem nostrum Ottonem Portuensem, tunc sancti Nicolai in Carcere Tulliano diaconum cardinalem, et bonae memoriae Iacobum Praenestinum episcopos, apostolicae sedis legatos, nobilia et magna ecclesiae Romanae membra, personaliter capi fecit et bonis omnibus spoliatos ac per diversa loca non semel ignominiose deductos carceribus mancipari.

Privilegium insuper, quod beato Petro et successoribus eius in ipso tradidit dominus Iesus Christus, videlicet: quodcumque ligaveris super terram, erit ligatum et in coelis, et quodcumque solveris super terram, erit solutum et in coelis, in quo utique auctoritas et potestas ecclesiae Romanae consistit, pro viribus diminuere vel ipsi ecclesiae auferre sategit, scribens se praefati Gregorii sententias non vereri, latam ab eo excommunicationem in ipsum non solum contemptis ecclesiae clavibus non servando, verum etiam per se ac officiales suos et illam et alias excommunicationis vel interdicti sententias, quas idem omnino contempsit, cogendo alios non servare.

Possessiones quoque praefatae Romanae ecclesiae, videlicet Marchiam, Ducatum, Beneventum, cuius muros et turres dirui fecit, ac alias quas in Tusciae ac Lombardiae partibus et quibusdam aliis obtinebat locis, paucis exceptis, occupare non metuens, eas adhuc detinet occupatas.

Et tamquam ei non sufficeret, quod manifeste contra iuramenta praemissa praesumendo talia veniebat, per se vel suos officiales earumdem possessionum homines deierare compulit, ipsos a iuramentis fidelitatis, quibus Romanae tenebantur ecclesiae, de facto, cum de iure non posset, absolvens et faciens eosdem fidelitatem nihilominus abiurare praedictam sibi que fidelitatis huiusmodi iuramenta praestare.

Pacis vero ipsum violatorem exsistere plene constat, quia cum olim tempore pacis inter ipsum et ecclesiam reformatae iurasset coram bonae memoriae Ioanni de Abbatis Villa episcopo Sabinensi et magistro Thomasio tituli sanctae Sabinae presbytero cardinali, praesentibus multis praelatis, principibus et baronibus, quod staret et pareret praecise absque ulla conditione omnibus mandatis ecclesiae super iis, pro quibus erat vinculo excommunicationis astrictus, causis excommunicationis eiusdem expressis per ordinem coram eo, tunc omnibus Theotonicis, hominibus regni Siciliae ac quibuslibet aliis, qui ecclesiae contra ipsum adhaeserant, omnem remittens offensam et poenam, et quod nullo tempore offenderet vel offendi faceret ipsos pro eo quod ecclesiae adstiterant, praestari in anima sua per Thomasium comitem Acerrarum faciens iuramentum, postmodum pacem et iuramenta huiusmodi, nequaquam erubescens irretiri periuriis, non servavit.

Nonnullos enim ex ipsis hominibus tam nobiles quam alios postea capi fecit et, eis bonis suis omnibus spoliatis, uxores eorum et filios captivari ac terras ecclesiae contra promissionem, quam eisdem Ioanni Sabinensi episcopo et Thomasio cardinali fecerat, irreverenter invasit, licet ipsi extunc in eum praesentem, si contraveniret, excommunicationis sententiam promulgarint.

Et cum iidem apostolica sibi auctoritate mandassent, ut nec per se nec per alium impediret, quin postulationes, electiones et confirmationes ecclesiarum et monasteriorum in regno praefato libere de cetero fierent secundum statuta concilii generalis, et quod nullus deinceps in eodem regno viris ecclesiasticis ac rebus eorum imponeret tallias vel collectas, quod que nullus ibidem clericus vel persona ecclesiastica de cetero in civili vel criminali causa conveniretur coram iudice saeculari, nisi super feudis quaestio civiliter haberetur, ac Templariis, Hospitalariis et aliis personis ecclesiasticis de damnis et iniuriis irrogatis eisdem satisfaceret competenter, ipse mandatum huiusmodi adimplere contempsit.

Liquet namque undecim aut plures archiepiscopales et multas episcopales sedes, abbatias quoque ac alias ecclesias vacare ad praesens in regno praedicto eas que procurante ipso, sicut aperte patet, fuisse diutius praelatorum regimine destitutas in grave ipsarum praeiudicium et periculum animarum.

Et licet forte in aliquibus eiusdem regni ecclesiis electiones sint a capitulis celebratae, quia tamen per illas eiusdem familiares clerici sunt electi, probabili potest argumento concludi, quod facultatem non habuerunt liberam eligendi.

Ecclesiarum autem ipsius regni non solum facultates et bona fecit prout voluit occupari, sed etiam cruces, turibula, calices et alios sacros earum thesauros et pannos sericos velut cultus divini contemptor auferri, licet ut dicitur ipsis ecclesiis, exacto tamen prius pro eis certo pretio, in parte fuerint restituti.

Clerici quippe collectis et talliis multipliciter affliguntur, nec solum trahuntur ad iudicium saeculare, sed ut asseritur coguntur subire duella, incarcerantur, occiduntur et patibulis cruciantur in confusionem et opprobrium ordinis clericalis.

Praefatis autem Templariis, Hospitalariis et personis ecclesiasticis non est de damnis illatis eisdem et iniuriis satisfactum.

Eum quoque certum est fore sacrilegii patratorem. Nam cum praefati Portuensis et Praenestinus episcopi et quam plures ecclesiarum praelati et clerici tam religiosi quam saeculares ad apostolicam sedem pro celebrando concilio, quod prius ipse petiverat, convocati per mare venirent, viis terrae ipsis de mandato eius omnino praeclusis, idem destinato Ensio filio suo cum multitudine galearum et per alias quamplures longe antea serio praeparatas in partibus Tusciae maritimis insidiis positis contra eos, ut gravius posset virus vomere praeconceptum, ipsos ausu sacrilego capi fecit, quibusdam praelatorum ipsorum et aliis in huiusmodi captione submersis, nonnullis etiam interemptis et aliquibus hostili insecutione fugatis, reliquis autem bonis spoliatis omnibus et de loco ad locum in regnum Siciliae opprobriose deductis ac ibidem diris carceribus mancipatis.

Quorum aliqui macerati squaloribus et inedia pressi miserabiliter defecerunt.

Merito insuper contra eum de haeretica pravitate suspicio est exorta, cum postquam excommunicationis sententiam a praefatis Ioanne episcopo Sabinensi et Thomasio cardinali prolatam incurrit et dictus Gregorius papa ipsum anathematis vinculo innodavit, ac post ecclesiae Romanae cardinalium, praelatorum et clericorum ac aliorum etiam diversis temporibus ad sedem apostolicam venientium captionem, claves ecclesiae contempserit et contemnat, sibi faciens celebrari vel potius quantum in eo est prophanari divina, et constanter asseveraverit, ut superius est narratum, se praefati Gregorii papae sententias non vereri.

Praeterea coniunctus amicitia detestabili Sarracenis, nuntios et munera pluries destinavit eisdem et ab eis vicissim cum honorificentia et ilaritate recepit ipsorum que ritus amplectitur, illos in cotidianis eius obsequiis notabiliter se cum tenens, eorumdem etiam more uxoribus quas habuit de stirpe regia descendentibus, eunuchos, praecipue quos, ut dicitur serio, castrari fecerat, non erubuit deputare custodes.

Et quod execrabilius est, olim exsistens in partibus transmarinis, facta compositione quadam, immo collusione verius cum soldano, Machometi nomen in templo Domini diebus et noctibus publice proclamari permisit.

Et nuper nuntios soldani Babiloniae, postquam idem soldanus Terrae sanctae ac christianis habitatoribus eius per se ac suos damna gravissima et inaestimabiles iniurias irrogarat, fecit per regnum Siciliae cum laudibus ad eiusdem soldani extollentiam, sicut fertur, honorifice suscipi et magnifice procurari.

Aliorum quoque infidelium perniciosis et horrendis obsequiis contra fideles abutens et illis qui damnabiliter vilipendentes apostolicam sedem ab unitate ecclesiae discesserunt, procurans affinitate ac amicitia copulari, clarae memoriae Ludovicum ducem Bavariae, specialem ecclesiae Romanae devotum, fecit, sicut pro certo asseritur, christiana religione despecta per assasinos occidi, et Batatio, Dei et ecclesiae inimico a communione fidelium per excommunicationis sententiam cum adiutoribus, consiliatoribus et fautoribus suis solemniter separato, filiam suam tradidit in uxorem.

Catholicorum vero principum actus et mores respuens, neglector salutis et famae, pietatis operibus non intendit.

Quin immo, ut de suis nefariis dissolutionibus sileamus, cum didicerit opprimere, non curat oppressos misericorditer relevare, manu eius, ut decet principem, ad eleemosynas non extenta, cum destructioni ecclesiarum institerit et religiosas ac alias ecclesiasticas iugi attriverit afflictione personas; nec ecclesias nec monasteria nec hospitalia seu alia pia loca cernitur construxisse.

Nonne igitur haec non levia, sed efficacia sunt argumenta de suspicione haeresis contra eum? cum tamen haereticorum vocabulo illos ius civile contineri asserat et latis adversus eos sententiis debere succumbere, qui vel levi argumento a iudicio catholicae religionis et tramite detecti fuerint deviare.

Praeter haec regnum Siciliae, quod est speciale patrimonium beati Petri et idem princeps ab apostolica sede tenebat in feudum, iam ad tantam in clericis et laicis exinanitionem servitutem que redegit, quod eis paene penitus nihil habentibus et omnibus exinde fere probis eiectis, illos qui remanserunt ibidem sub servili quasi conditione vivere ac Romanam ecclesiam, cuius principaliter sunt homines et vassalli, offendere multipliciter et hostiliter impugnare compellit.

Posset etiam merito reprehendi, quod mille squifatorum annuam pensionem, in qua pro eodem regno ipsi ecclesiae Romanae tenetur, per novem annos et amplius solvere praetermisit.

Nos itaque super praemissis et quam pluribus aliis eius nefandis excessibus cum fratribus nostris et sacro concilio deliberatione praehabita diligenti, cum Iesu Christi vices licet immeriti teneamus in terris nobis que in beati Petri apostoli persona sit dictum: quodcumque ligaveris super terram et cetera, memoratum principem, qui se imperio et regnis omni que honore ac dignitate reddidit tam indignum, qui que propter suas iniquitates a Deo ne regnet vel imperet est abiectus, suis ligatum peccatis et abiectum omni que honore ac dignitate privatum a Domino ostendimus, denuntiamus ac nihilominus sententiando privamus, omnes qui ei iuramento fidelitatis tenentur adstricti, a iuramento huiusmodi perpetuo absolventes, auctoritate apostolica firmiter inhibendo, ne quisquam de cetero sibi tamquam imperatori vel regi pareat vel intendat, et decernendo quoslibet, qui deinceps ei velut imperatori aut regi consilium vel auxilium praestiterint seu favorem, ipso facto excommunicationis vinculo subiacere.

Illi autem, ad quos in eodem imperio imperatoris spectat electio, eligant libere successorem.

De praefato vero Siciliae regno providere curabimus cum eorumdem fratrum nostrorum consilio, sicut viderimus expedire.

Da(tum) Lugduni, XVI. Kal(endas) augusti, pontificatus nostri anno tertio.

Cum in multis iuris articulis infinitas reprobetur provide duximus statuendum ut per generalem clausulam quidam alii quae frequenter in litteris nostris inseritur ultra tres vel quatuor in iudicium non trahantur.

Quorum nomina in primo citatorio exprimat impetrator ne fraudi locus forsitan relinquatur si circa ea possit libere variare.

Praesenti decreto duximus providendum ne a sede apostolica vel legatis ipsius causae aliquibus committantur nisi personis quae vel dignitate sint praeditae vel in ecclesiis cathedralibus seu aliis collegiatis honorabilibus institutae nec alibi quam in civitatibus vel locis magnis et insignibus ubi haberi valeat iuris copia peritorum causae huiusmodi agitentur.

Iudicibus vero qui contra hoc statutum ad alia loca alterutram partium citaverint vel utramque non pareatur impune nisi citatio de communi utriusque partis processerit voluntate.

Dispendia litium aequitatis compendio volentes qua possumus industria coarctare statutum felicis recordationis Innocentii papae tertii super hoc editum ampliantes decrevimus ut si quis contra alium plures personales movere voluerit quaestiones non ad diversos iudices sed ad eosdem super omnibus huiusmodi quaestionibus litteras studeat impetrare.

Qui vero contrarium fecerit omni commodo careat litterarum nec processus valeat habitus per easdem alias si eum per ipsas fatigaverit in expensis legitimis condemnetur.

Reus quoque si eodem durante iudicio actorem sibi obnoxium dixerit reconventionis beneficio vel conventionis si litteras contra eum impetrare maluerit de iure suo debet apud eosdem iudices experiri nisi eos ut suspectos poterit recusare simili poena si contrafecerit puniendus.

Statuimus ut si quis electionem postulationem vel provisionem factam impugnat in formam obiciens aliquid vel personam et propter hoc ad nos appellari contingat tam is qui opponit quam qui defendit et generaliter omnes quorum interest et quos causa contingit per se vel per procuratores ad causam instructos ad sedem apostolicam a die obiectionis iter arripiant infra mensem.

Sed si pars aliqua non venerit post viginti dies post adventum alterius partis exspectata in electionis negotio non obstante cuiusquam absentia sicut de iure fuerit procedetur.

Haec autem in dignitatibus personatibus et canonicis observari volumus et mandamus.

Adicimus etiam ut qui non plene probaverit quod in forma opponit ad expensas quas propter hoc pars altera fecisse docuerit condemnetur.

Qui vero in probatione defecerit eius quod in personam obicit a beneficiis ecclesiasticis triennio noverit se suspensum.

Atque si infra illud tempus propria se temeritate ingesserit tunc illis ipso iure perpetuo sit privatus nullam super hoc de misericordia spem aut fiduciam habiturus nisi manifestissimis constiterit documentis quod ipsum a calumniae vitio causa probabilis et sufficiens excuset.

In electionibus et postulationibus ac scrutiniis ex quibus ius oritur eligendi vota conditionalia alternativa et incerta penitus reprobamus statuentes ut huiusmodi votis pro non adiectis habitis ex puris consensibus celebretur electio voce illorum qui non pure consenserint ea vice in alios recidente. Statuimus ut conservatores quos plerumque concedimus a manifestis iniuriis et violentiis defendere possint quos eis committimus defendendos nec ad alia quae iudicialem indaginem exigunt suam valeant extendere potestatem.

Officii nostri debitum remediis invigilat subiectorum quia dum eorum excutimus onera dum scandala removemus nos in ipsorum quiete quiescimus et fovemur in pace.

Proinde praesenti decreto statuimus ut ecclesiae Romanae legati quantumcumque plenam legationem obtineant sive a nobis missi fuerint sive suarum ecclesiarum praetextu legationis sibi vendicent dignitatem ex ipsius legationis munere conferendi beneficia nullam habeant potestatem nisi hoc alicui specialiter duxerimus indulgendum.

Quod tamen in fratribus nostris legatione fungentibus nolumus observari quia sicut honoris praerogativa laetantur sic eos auctoritate fungi volumus ampliori.

Iuris esse ambiguum non videtur iudicem delegatum qui a sede apostolica ad hoc mandatum non receperit speciale iubere non posse alterutram partium coram se personaliter in iudicio comparere nisi causa fuerit criminalis vel nisi pro veritate dicenda vel iuramento calumniae faciendo iuris necessitas partes coram eo personaliter exegerit praesentari.

Exceptionis peremptoriae seu defensionis cuiuslibet principalis cognitionem negotii continentis ante litem contestatam obiectus nisi de re iudicata vel transacta seu finita excipiat litigator litis contestationem fieri non impediat nec retardet licet dicat obiector non fuisse rescriptum obtentum si quae sunt impetranti opposita fuissent exposita deleganti.

Frequens et assidua nos querela circumstrepit quod spoliationis exceptio nonnumquam in iudiciis calumniose proposita causas ecclesiasticas impedit et perturbat.

Dum enim exceptioni insistitur appellationes interponi contingit.

Et sic intermittitur et plerumque perimitur causae cognitio principalis.

Et propterea nos qui voluntarios labores appetimus ut quietem aliis praeparemus finem litibus cupientes imponi et calumniae materiam amputari statuimus ut in civilibus negotiis spoliationis obiectione quae ab alio quam ab actore facta proponitur iudex in principali procedere non postponat.

Sed si in civilibus ab actore in criminalibus autem se spoliatum reus asserat a quocumque infra quindecim dierum spatium post diem in quo proponitur quod asseruit comprobabit alioquin in expensis quas actor interim ob hoc fecerit iudiciali taxatione praehabita condemnetur.

Alias si aequum iudici visum fuerit puniendus.

Illum autem spoliatum intelligi volumus in hoc casu cum criminaliter accusatur qui tota substantia sua vel maiori parte ipsius per violentiam se destitutum affirmat.

Et secundum hoc loqui canones sano credendum est intellectu quia nec nudi contendere nec inermes inimicis opponere non debemus.

Habet enim spoliatus privilegium ut non possit exui iam nudatus.

Solet autem inter scholasticos dubitari si spoliatus a tertio de spoliatione contra suum accusatorem excipiat an ei tempus a iudice debeat indulgeri infra quod restitutionem imploret.

Ne forte sic velit exsistere ut omnem accusatorem eludat quod satis aequitati consonum aestimamus.

Et si infra tempus indultum restitutionem non petierit et causam cum potuerit non perduxerit ad finem non obstante spoliationis exceptione deinceps poterit accusari.

Ad haec sancimus ut rerum privatarum spoliatio agenti super ecclesiasticis vel e nullatenus apponatur.

Actor qui venire ad terminum ad quem citari adversarium fecerat non curavit venienti reo in expensis propter hoc factis legitime condemnetur ad citationem aliam nisi sufficienter caveat quod in termino compareat minime admittendus.

Eum qui super dignitate personatu vel beneficio ecclesiastico obtinendis cum alio litigat possessore ob partis adversae contumaciam causa rei servandae in ipsorum possessionem statuimus non mittendum ne per hoc ad ea ingressus patere valeat vitiosus sed liceat in hoc casu contumacis absentiam divina replente praesentia etiam lite non contestata diligenter examinato negotio ipsum fine debito terminare.

Statuimus ut positiones negativas quae probari non possunt nisi per confessionem adversarii iudices admittere possint si aequitate suadente viderint expedire.

Pia consideratione statuit mater ecclesia quod maioris excommunicationis exceptio in quacumque parte iudiciorum opposita lites differat et repellat agentes ut ex hoc magis censura ecclesiastica timeatur et communionis periculum evitetur contumaciae vitium reprimatur et excommunicati dum a communibus actibus excluduntur rubore suffusi ad humilitatis gratiam et reconciliationis effectum facilius inclinentur.

Sed hominum succrescente malitia quod provisum est ad remedium transit ad noxas.

Dum enim in causis ecclesiasticis frequentius haec exceptio per malitiam opponatur contingit differri negotia et partes fatigari laboribus et expensis.

Proinde quia morbus iste quasi communis irrepsit dignum duximus communem adhibere medelam.

Si quis igitur excommunicationem opponat speciem ipsius et nomen excommunicatoris exponat sciturus eam rem se deferre in publicam notionem quam infra octo dierum spatium die in quo proponitur minime computato probare valeat apertissimis documentis.

Quod si non probaverit iudex in causa procedere non omittat reum in expensis quas actor ob hoc diebus illis se fecisse docuerit praehabita taxatione condemnans.

Si vero postmodum instantia durante iudicii et probandi copia succedente de eadem excommunicatione vel alia excipiatur iterum et probetur actor in sequentibus excludatur donec meruerit absolutionis gratiam obtinere his quae praecesserunt nihilominus in suo robore duraturis.

Proviso ut ultra duas vices non haec proponatur exceptio praeterquam si excommunicatio nova emerserit vel evidens et prompta probatio supervenerit de antiqua. Sed si post rem iudicatam talis exceptio proponatur executionem impediet sed sententia quae praecessit non minus robur debitum obtinebit eo tamen salvo ut si actor excommunicatus sit publice et hoc iudex noverit quandocumque etsi de hoc reus non excipiat iudex actorem ex suo officio repellere non postponat.

Cum aeterni principis tribunal illum reum non habeat quem iniuste iudex condemnat testante propheta nec damnabit eum cum iudicabitur illi caveant ecclesiastici iudices et prudenter attendant ut in causarum processibus nihil vendicet odium nihil vel favor usurpet timor exsulet praemium aut expectatio praemii iustitiam non evertat.

Sed stateram gestent in manibus lances appendant aequo libramine ut in omnibus quae in causis agenda fuerint praesertim in concipiendis sententiis et ferendis prae oculis habeant solum deum illius imitantes exemplum qui querelas populi tabernaculum ingressus ad dominum referebat ut secundum eius imperium iudicaret.

Si quis autem iudex ecclesiasticus ordinarius aut delegatus famae prodigus et proprii persecutor honoris contra conscientiam et contra iustitiam in gravamen partis alterius in iudicio quicquam fecerit per gratiam vel per sordes ab executione officii per annum noverit se suspensum ad aestimationem litis parti quam laeserit nihilominus condemnandus sciturus quod si suspensione durante damnabiliter ingesserit se divinis irregularitatis laqueo se involvet secundum canonicas sanctiones a quo nonnisi per sedem poterit apostolicam liberari salvis aliis constitutionibus quae iudicibus male iudicantibus poenas gerunt et infligunt.

Dignum est etenim ut qui in tot praesumit offendere poena multiplici castigetur.

Cordi nobis est lites minuere et a laboribus relevare subiectos.

Sancimus igitur ut si quis in iudicio vel extra super interlocutoria vel gravamine ad nos duxerit appellandum causam appellationis in scriptis assignare deproperet petens apostolos quos ei praecipimus exhiberi.

In quibus appellationis causam iudex exprimat et cur appellatio non sit admissa vel si appellationi forsitan ex superioris reverentia sit delatum.

Post haec appellatori secundum locorum distantiam personarum et negotii qualitatem tempore prosecutionis indulto si appellatus voluerit et principales petierint per se vel per procuratores instructos cum mandato ad agendum rationibus et munimentis ad causam spectantibus accedant ad sedem apostolicam sic parati ut si nobis visum fuerit expedire finito appellationis articulo vel partium voluntati comisso procedatur in negotio principali quantum poterit et de iure debebit his quae in appellationibus a definitivis sententiis interpositis antiquitas statuit non mutatis.

Quod si appellator quae praemissa sunt non observet reputabitur non appellans et ad prioris iudicis redibit examen in expensis legitimis condemnandus.

Si autem appellatus contempserit hoc statutum in eum tamquam contumacem tam in expensis quam in causa quantum a iure permittitur procedatur.

Iustum est equidem ut in eum iura consurgant qui ius iudicem et partem eludit.

Legitima suspicionis causa contra iudicem assignata et arbitris a partibus secundum formam iuris electis qui de ipsa cognoscant saepe contingit quod ipsis in idem convenire nolentibus nec tertium advocantibus cum quo ambo vel alter eorum procedant ad decisionem ipsius negotii ut tenentur iudex proferat excommunicationis sententiam contra eos quam ipsi tum propter odium tum propter favorem diutius vilipendunt.

Quare causa ipsa plus debito prorogata non proceditur ad cognitionem negotii principalis.

Volentes igitur morbo huiusmodi necessariam adhibere medelam statuimus ut ipsis arbitris per iudicem competens terminus praefigatur infra quem in idem conveniant vel tertium concorditer advocent cum quo ambo vel alter ipsorum eiusdem suspicionis negotium terminare procurent.

Alioquin iudex extunc in principali negotio procedere non omittat.

Pro humani redemptione generis de summis coelorum ad ima mundi descendens et mortem tandem subiens temporalem dei filius Iesus Christus ne gregem sui pretio sanguinis gloriosi redemptum ascensurus post resurrectionem ad patrem absque pastore desereret ipsius curam beato Petro apostolo ut suae stabilitate fidei ceteros in christiana religione firmaret eorum que mentes ad salutis suae opera accenderet devotionis ardore commisit.

Unde nos eiusdem apostoli effecti disponente domino licet immeriti successores et ipsius redemptoris locum in terris quamquam indigne tenentes circa gregis eiusdem custodiam sollicitis excitari vigiliis et animarum saluti iugis accensione cogitationis intendere submovendo noxia et agendo profutura debemus ut excusso a nobis negligentiae somno nostri que cordis oculis diligentia sedula vigilantibus animas ipsas deo lucrifacere sua nobis cooperante gratia valeamus.

Cum igitur illi qui sic horrenda inhumanitate detestanda que saevitia mortem sitiunt aliorum ut ipsos faciant per assassinos occidi non solum corporum sed mortem procurent etiam animarum nisi eas exuberans gratia divina praevenerit ut sint armis spiritualibus praemuniti ac omnis potestas tribuatur a domino ad iustitiam rectum que iudicium exercendum nos tanto periculo volentes occurrere animarum et tam nefarios praesumptores ecclesiasticae animadversionis mucrone ferire ut metus poenae meta huiusmodi praesumptionis exsistat praesertim cum nonnulli magnates taliter perimi formidantes coacti fuerint securitatem ab eorumdem assasinorum domino impetrare sic que.

Ab eo non absque christianae dignitatis opprobrio redimere quodammodo vitam suam sacri concilii approbatione statuimus ut quicumque princeps praelatus seu quaelibet alia ecclesiastica seu saecularis persona quempiam christianorum per praedictos assasinos interfici fecerit vel etiam mandaverit quamquam mors ex hoc forsitan non prosequatur aut eos receptaverit vel defenderit seu occultaverit excommunicationis et depositionis a dignitate honore ordine officio et beneficio incurrat sententias ipso facto et ista libere aliis per illos ad quos illorum collatio pertinet conferantur.

Sit etiam cum suis bonis mundanis omnibus tamquam christianae religionis aemulus a toto christiano populo perpetuo diffidatus et postquam probabilibus constiterit documentis aliquod scelus tam execrabile commisisse nullatenus alia excommunicationis vel depositionis seu diffidationis adversus eum sententia requiratur.

Cum medicinalis sit excommunicatio non mortalis disciplinans non eradicans dum tamen is in quem lata fuerit non contemnat caute provideat iudex ecclesiasticus ut in ea ferenda ostendat se prosequi quod corrigentis est et medentis.

Quisquis ergo excommunicat in scriptis proferat et causam expresse conscribat propter quam excommunicatio proferatur.

Exemplum vero scripturae huiusmodi teneatur excommunicato tradere infra mensem post diem sententiae si fuerit requisitus.

Super qua requisitione fieri volumus publicum instrumentum vel literas testimoniales confici sigillo authentico consignatas.

Si quis autem iudicum huiusmodi constitutionis temerarius violator exsistat per mensem unum ab ingressu ecclesiae et divinis noverit se suspensum.

Superior vero ad quem recurritur sententiam ipsam sine difficultate relaxans latorem excommunicationis ad expensas et omne interesse condemnet vel alias puniat animadversione condigna ut poena docente discant iudices quam grave sit excommunicationis sententias sine maturitate debita fulminare.

Et haec eadem in suspensionis et interdicti sententiis volumus observari.

Caveant autem ecclesiarum praelati et iudices universi ne praedictam suspensionis poenam incurrant.

Quod si contigerit eos divina officia prosequi sicut prius irregularitatem non effugiant iuxta canonicas sanctiones super qua nonnisi per summum pontificem poterit dispensari. Solet a nonnullis in dubium revocari an cum aliquis per superiorem absolvi postulat ad cautelam dum in se latam excommunicationis sententiam asserit esse nullam sine contradictionis obstaculo munus ei debeat absolutionis impendi et an ante absolutionem huiusmodi qui se offert in iudicio probaturum se post appellationem legitimam excommunicatione innodatum vel intolerabilem errorem in sententia fuisse patenter expressum sit in ceteris excepto probationis illius articulo evitandus.

In prima igitur dubitatione sic statuimus observandum ut petenti absolutio non negetur quamvis in hoc excommunicator vel adversarius se opponat nisi eum excommunicatum pro manifesta dicat offensa in quo casu terminus octo dierum indulgebitur sic dicenti.

Ut si probaverit quod opponit nec relaxetur sententia nisi prius sufficiens praestetur emenda vel competens cautio de parendo si offensa dubia proponatur.

In secunda vero quaestione statuimus ut is qui ad probandum admittitur pendente probationis articulo in ceteris quae ut actor in iudiciis acceptaverit interim evitetur extra iudicium vero in officiis postulationibus et electionibus et aliis legitimis actibus nihilominus admittatur.

Statuimus ut nullus iudicum participantes cum excommunicatis ab eo in locutione et aliis quibus ligatur participans excommunicatione minori ante commonitionem canonicam excommunicare maiori praesumat salvis constitutionibus contra illos legitime promulgatis qui in crimine praesumunt participare damnato.

Quod si ex locutione et aliis quibus participans labitur in minorem excommunicaturus fortius indurescat poterit iudex post commonitionem canonicam huiusmodi participantes consimili damnare censura.

Aliter autem in participantes excommunicatio prolata non teneat et proferentes poenam legitimam poterunt formidare.

Quia periculosum est episcopis et eorum superioribus propter executionem pontificalis officii quod frequenter incumbit ut in aliquo casu interdicti vel suspensionis incurrant sententiam ipso facto nos deliberatione provida duximus statuendum ut episcopi et alii superiores praelati nullius constitutionis occasione sententiae seu mandati praedictam incurrant sententiam nullatenus ipso iure nisi in ipsis de episcopis et superioribus expressim mentio habeatur.

Huic etiam adicimus sanctioni ut illud quod in constitutione solet a nonnullis a nobis hactenus promulgata fuerat constitutum ut cum aliquis se offert in iudicio probaturum post appellationem legitimam excommunicationis se sententia innodatum pendente probationis articulo in iis quae extra iudicium agitantur electionibus postulationibus officiis ac aliis actibus legitimis non debeat evitari ad episcoporum et archiepiscoporum sententias nullatenus extendatur sed illud obtineat in futurum quod olim in talibus actibus exstitit observatum.

Cura nos pastoralis sollicitat et hortatur ut lapsis consulamus ecclesiis et ne labantur in posterum provideamus constitutione salubri.

Cum igitur usurarum vorago multas ecclesias paene destruxerit et nonnulli praelati circa solutionem debitorum praesertim a suis praedecessoribus contractorum negligentes inveniantur admodum et remissi ac ad contrahenda maiora debita et obligandas res ecclesiae nimis proni desides etiam in custodiendis rebus inventis malentes in propriam laudem modicum novi facere quam bona custodire dimissa recuperare deperdita restaurare ac resarcire ruinas nos ne de cetero se de administratione minus utili excusare ac in praedecessores sive alios fundere valeant culpam suam praesentis concilii approbatione sancimus ut pontifices abbates decani ceteri que legitimam et communem administrationem gerentes infra unum mensem postquam administrationem adierint intimato prius proximo superiori ut per se.

Vel per aliquam personam ecclesiasticam idoneam et fidelem intersit praesentibus que capitulo vel conventu propter hoc specialiter evocatis inventarium rerum administrationis susceptae confici faciant in quo mobilia et immobilia libri chartae instrumenta privilegia ornamenta seu paramenta ecclesiastica et cuncta quae ad instructionem urbani fundi seu rustici pertinent necnon debita ac credita diligentissime conscribantur ut in quo statu ecclesiam vel administrationem susceperint et procedente tempore gubernarint ac in morte vel cessione dimiserint per superiorem si necesse fuerit et eos qui sunt ecclesiarum deputati servitiis liquido cognoscatur.

Archiepiscopi vero qui praeter Romanum pontificem superiorem non habent aliquem ex suffraganeis ut personaliter vel per alium ut est expressum superius et abbates ac alii praelati minores exempti unum vicinum episcopum qui nihil iuris in exempta ecclesia sibi vindicet ad id studeant evocare dictum que inventarium tam substituti praelati quam sui collegii necnon et superioris suffraganei seu vicini episcopi ad hoc vocatorum muniatur sigillis in archivis ecclesiae cum cautela debita conservandum et nihilominus inventarii eiusdem transcriptum tam idem institutus quam praelatus ad hoc vocatus penes se habeat simile sigillatum.

Inventa quoque custodiantur fideliter et de ipsis administratio digna geratur et comperta debita de mobilibus ecclesiae si fieri potest cum celeritate solvantur.

Si vero mobilia non sufficiant ad solutionem celerem faciendam omnes proventus in solutionem convertantur debitorum quae usuraria fuerint vel etiam onerosa deductis de ipsis proventibus expensis dumtaxat necessariis praelato collegio que rationabiliter computandis.

Si autem debita non fuerint onerosa vel usuraria tertia pars eorundem proventuum vel maior cum illorum consilio quos ad conficiendum inventarium vocandos diximus pro satisfactione huiusmodi deputentur.

Porro eiusdem concilii auctoritate firmiter inhibemus ne praedicti personas suas vel ecclesias sibi commissas pro aliis obligent nec pro se vel ipsis ecclesiis contrahant debita quibus possit imminere gravamen.

Si vero evidens urgeat necessitas vel ecclesiarum rationabilis suadeat utilitas praelati cum superiorum archiepiscopi et abbates exempti cum praedictorum collegiorum que suorum concilio et consensu debita non usuraria si potest fieri nunquam tamen in nundinis vel mercatis publicis contrahant et contractuum litteris debitorum et creditorum nomina et causas quare contrahatur debitum etiam si in utilitatem ecclesiae sit conversum et ad id personas ecclesiasticas vel ecclesias nullatenus volumus obligari.

Privilegia siquidem ecclesiarum quae securo loco fideliter custodiri mandamus nequaquam pignori obligentur nec etiam res aliae nisi forte pro necessariis et utilibus debitis cum praedicta solemnitate contractis.

Ut autem haec salubris constitutio inviolabiliter observetur et fructus appareat quem ex ipsa provenire speramus ordinandum duximus et irrefragabiliter statuendum quod omnes abbates et priores necnon et decani vel praepositi cathedralium seu aliarum ecclesiarum semel saltem in anno in ipsorum collegiis districtam suae administrationis faciant rationem et coram superiore visitante conscripta et consignata huiusmodi ratio fideliter recitetur.

Archiepiscopi vero et episcopi statum administrationis bonorum ad mensam propriam pertinentium similiter singulis annis capitulis suis et nihilominus episcopi metropolitanis et metropolitani legatis apostolicae sedis vel aliis quibus fuerit ab eadem sede suarum ecclesiarum visitatio delegata insinuare debita fidelitate procurent.

Computationes vero conscriptae semper in thesauro ecclesiae ad memoriam reserventur ut in computatione annorum sequentium praeteriti temporis et instantis diligens habeatur collatio ex qua superior administrantis diligentiam vel negligentiam comprehendat quam siquidem negligentiam solum deum habens prae oculis hominis amore odio vel timore postpositis tanta et tali animadversione castiget quod nec a deo nec a suo superiori vel sede apostolica mereatur propter hoc recipere ultionem.

Non solum autem a futuris praelatis sed etiam a iam promotis praesentem constitutionem praecipimus observari.

Arduis mens nostra occupata negotiis curis que distracta diversis inter cetera circa quae attentionis invigilat oculo ad constantinopolitani liberationem imperii suae considerationis aciem specialiter dirigit hanc ardenti desiderio concupiscit erga eam iugi cogitatione versatur et licet apostolica sedes pro ipsa grandis diligentiae studio et multiplicis subventionis remedio ferventer institerit ac diu catholici non sine gravibus laboribus et onerosis sumptibus anxiis que sudoribus et deflenda sanguinis effusione certarint nec tanti auxilii dextera imperium ipsum totaliter de inimicorum iugo potuerit impedientibus peccatis eripere propter quod non immerito dolore turbamur.

Quia tamen ecclesiae corpus ex membris causa cari videlicet imperii praefati carentia notam probrosae deformitatis incurreret et sustineret debilitatis dolendae iacturam posset que digne nostrae ac ipsius ecclesiae desidiae imputari si fidelium destitueretur suffragio et relinqueretur hostibus libere opprimendum firma intentione proponimus eidem imperio efficaci et celeri subsidio subvenire ut ecclesia ferventi ad illius exurgente succursum manum que porrigente munitam imperium ipsum de adversariorum dominio erui valeat et reduci auctore domino ad eiusdem corporis unitatem sentiat que post conterentem inimicorum malleum dexteram matris ecclesiae consolantem et post assertionis erroneae caecitatem visum catholicae fidei possessione resumat.

Ad liberationem autem ipsius eo magis ecclesiarum praelatos alios que viros ecclesiasticos vigiles et intentos exsistere ac opem et operam convenit exhibere quo amplius eiusdem fidei et ecclesiasticae libertatis augmentum quod per liberationem huiusmodi principaliter proveniret procurare tenentur.

Maxime quia dum praedicto subvenitur imperio consequenter subsidium impenditur terrae sanctae.

Sane ut festina fiat et utilis imperio praefato subventio ex communi concilii approbatione statuimus ut medietas omnium proventuum tam dignitatum et personatuum quam praebendarum ecclesiasticarum aliorum que beneficiorum ecclesiasticarum personarum illarum quae in ipsis residentiam non faciunt personalem per sex menses ad minus sive unum habeant sive plura eis qui nostris et fratrum nostrorum ac suorum praelatorum immorantur obsequiis aut sunt in peregrinatione vel scholis seu ecclesiarum suarum negotia de ipsorum mandato procurant aut assumpserunt vel assument crucis signaculum in praedictae terrae vel personaliter in eiusdem imperii proficiscentur succursum exceptis et si.

Aliqui eorundem exceptorum praeter huiusmodi crucesignatos et proficiscentes de reditibus ecclesiasticis ultra valentiam centum marcarum argenti percipiunt annuatim tertia pars residui ipsius imperii subsidio colligenda per eos qui ad hoc apostolica fuerint ordinati providentia usque ad triennium integre deputentur non obstantibus quibuscumque consuetudinibus vel statutis ecclesiarum seu quibuslibet indulgentiis ipsis ecclesiis vel personis ab apostolica sede concessis iuramento aut quacunque firmitate alia roboratis.

Et si forte super hoc fraudem scienter commiserint sententiam excommunicationis incurrant. Nos vero de obventionibus ecclesiae Romanae deducta prius ex eis decima succursu terrae deputanda praedictae decimam pro dicti subventione imperii plenarie tribuemus.

Porro cum idem iuvatur imperium auxilium praestatur potissime ipsi terrae ac ad recuperationem eius praecipue insistitur dum ad ipsius liberationem imperii laboratur de omnipotentis dei misericordia et beatorum Petri et Pauli apostolorum eius auctoritate confisi ex illa quam nobis licet indignis ligandi atque solvendi contulit potestate omnibus eidem imperio succurrentibus illam suorum peccaminum veniam indulgemus ipsos que illo privilegio ea que volumus immunitate gaudere quae praedictae terrae subvenientibus concedentur.

Perennis obtentu patriae a longis retro temporibus pro redimenda terra quam dei filius aspersione sui sanguinis consecravit universitas filiorum ecclesiae non solum expensas innumeras sed inaestimabilem cruoris affluentiam noscitur effudisse sicut ex eo moesti corde colligimus quod pridem contra fideles pugnantibus impiis accidit in partibus transmarinis.

Verum cum propter hoc sit in sedis apostolicae voto potissimum ut de ipsius redemptione terrae communis desiderii cito deo propitio proveniat complementum digne providimus ut ad procurandum dei favorem negotio vos nostris litteris excitemus.

Rogamus itaque universos vos et obsecramus in domino Iesu Christo mandantes quatenus singuli vestrum fideles populos vestrae curae commissos in vestris praedicationibus vel quando poenitentiam ipsis iniungitis piis monitis inducatis concessa super hoc prout expedire videritis indulgentia speciali ut in testamentis quae pro tempore fecerint aliquid in terrae sanctae vel imperii Romaniae subsidium pro suorum peccaminum remissione relinquant attentius provisuri ut quod ipsi ad crucifixi reverentiam habendo respectum in pecunia pro huiusmodi subventione dederint in certis locis sub sigillis vestris conservari fideliter et illa quae in rebus aliis ad hoc legata fuerint diligenter in scriptis redigi faciatis.

Hoc autem pietatis opus in quo sola causa dei quaeritur et salus fidelium procuratur sic vestra sinceritas promptis prosequatur affectibus ut tandem securi de manu superni iudicis caelestis gloriae praemium expectetis.

Christianae religionis cultum longius latius que per orbem diffundi super omnia cupientes inaestimabilis doloris telo transfodimur si quando aliqui sic nostro in hac parte obviant desiderio affectu contrario et effectu quod ipsum cultum delere penitus de terrae superficie omni studio tota que potentia moliuntur.

Sane Tartarorum gens impia christianum populum subiugare sibi vel potius perimere appetens collectis iam dudum suarum viribus nationum Poloniam Rusciam Ungariam alias que christianorum regiones ingressa sic in eas depopulatrix insaevit ut gladio eius nec aetati parcente nec sexui sed in omnes indifferenter crudelitate horribili debacchante inaudito ipsas exterminio devastarit ac aliorum regna continuato progressu illa sibi eodem in vagina otiari gladio nesciente incessabili persecutione substernit ut subsequenter in robore fortiores exercitus christianos invadens suam plenius in ipsos possit saevitiam exercere sic que orbato quod absit fidelibus orbe fides exorbitet dum sublatos sibi gemuerit ipsius gentis feritate cultores.

Ne igitur tam detestanda gentis eiusdem intentio proficere valeat sed deficiat auctore deo potius et contrario concludatur eventu ab universis christicolis attenta est consideratione pensandum et procurandum studio diligenti ut sic illius impediatur processus quod nequeat ad ipsos ulterius quantumcumque potenti armato brachio pertransire.

Ideo que sacro suadente concilio universos vos monemus rogamus et hortamur attente mandantes quatenus viam et aditus unde in terram nostram gens ipsa posset ingredi solertissime perscrutantes illos fossatis et muris seu aliis aedificiis aut artificiis prout expedire videritis taliter praemunire curetis quod eiusdem gentis ad vos ingressus patere de facili nequeat.

Sed prius apostolicae sedi suus denuntiari possit adventus ut ea vobis fidelium destinante succursum contra conatus et insultus gentis ipsius tuti esse adiutore domino valeatis.

Nos enim in tam necessariis et utilibus expensis quas ob id feceritis contribuemus magnifice ac ab omnibus christianorum regionibus cum per hoc occurratur communibus periculis proportionaliter contribui faciemus et nihilominus super his aliis christifidelibus per quorum partes habere posset aditum gens praedicta litteras praesentibus similes destinamus.

Afflicti corde pro deplorandis terrae sanctae periculis sed pro illis praecipue quae constitutis in ipsa fidelibus noscuntur noviter accidisse ad liberandum ipsam deo propitio de impiorum manibus totis affectibus aspiramus diffinientes sacro approbante concilio ut ita crucesignati se praeparent quod opportuno tempore universis insinuando fidelibus per praedicatores et nostros nuntios speciales omnes qui disposuerint transfretare in locis idoneis ad hoc conveniant.

De quibus in eiusdem terrae subsidium cum divina et apostolica benedictione procedant.

Sacerdotes autem et alii clerici qui fuerint in exercitu christiano tam subditi quam praelati orationi et exhortationi diligenter insistant docentes eos verbo pariter et exemplo ut timorem et amorem domini semper habeant ante oculos ne quid dicant aut faciant quod aeterni regis maiestatem offendat.

Et si quando in peccatum lapsi fuerint per veram poenitentiam mox resurgant gerentes humilitatem cordis et corporis et tam in victu quam in vestitu mediocritatem servantes dissensiones et aemulationes omnino vitando rancore ac livore a se penitus relegatis ut sic spiritualibus et materialibus armis muniti adversus hostes fidei securius praelientur non de sua praesumentes potentia sed de divina virtute sperantes.

Nobiles quidem et potentes exercitus ac omnes divitiis abundantes piis praelatorum monitis inducantur ut intuitu crucifixi pro quo crucis signaculum assumpserunt ab expensis inutilibus et superfluis sed ab illis praecipue quae fiunt in comessationibus et conviviis abstinentes eas commutent in personarum illarum subsidium per quas dei negotium valeat prosperari et eis propter hoc iuxta praelatorum ipsorum providentiam peccatorum suorum indulgentia tribuatur.

Praedictis autem clericis indulgemus ut beneficia sua integre percipiant per triennium ac essent in ecclesiis residentes et si necesse fuerit ea per idem tempus valeant pignori obligare.

Ne igitur hoc sanctum propositum impediri vel retardari contingat universis ecclesiarum praelatis districte praecipimus ut singuli per loca sua illos qui signum crucis deposuerunt resumere ac tam ipsos quam alios crucesignatos et quos adhuc signari contigerit ad reddendum domino vota sua diligentius moneant et inducant et si necesse fuerit per excommunicationis in personas et interdicti sententias in terras ipsorum omni tergiversatione cessante compellant.

Ad haec ne quid in negotio Iesu Christi de contingentibus omittatur volumus et mandamus ut patriarchae archiepiscopi episcopi abbates et alii qui curam obtinent animarum studiose proponant commissis sibi populis verbum crucis obsecrantes per patrem et filium et spiritum sanctum unum solum verum aeternum deum reges duces principes marchiones comites et barones alios que magnates necnon communia civitatum villarum et oppidorum ut qui personaliter non accesserint in subsidium terrae sanctae competentem conferant numerum bellatorum cum expensis ad triennium necessariis secundum proprias facultates in remissionem suorum peccaminum prout in generalibus litteris quas pridem per orbem terrae misimus est expressum et ad maiorem cautelam inferius etiam exprimetur.

Huius enim remissionis volumus esse participes non solum eos qui ad hoc naves proprias exhibebunt sed illos etiam qui propter hoc opus naves studuerint fabricare.

Renuentibus autem si qui forte tam ingrati fuerint domino deo nostro ex parte apostolica firmiter protestemur ut se sciant super hoc nobis in novissimo districti examinis die coram tremendo iudice responsuros prius tamen considerantes qua scientia qua ve securitate comparere poterunt coram unigenito dei filio Iesu Christo cui omnia dedit pater in manus si ei pro peccatoribus crucifixo servire renuerint in hoc negotio quasi proprie sibi proprio cuius munere vivunt cuius beneficio sustentantur quin etiam cuius sanguine sunt redempti.

Ceterum ex communi concilii approbatione statuimus ut omnes omnino clerici tam subditi quam praelati vigesimam ecclesiarum proventuum usque ad triennium integre conferant in subsidium terrae sanctae per manus eorum qui ad hoc apostolica fuerint providentia ordinati quibusdam dumtaxat religiosis exceptis ab hac praestatione merito eximendis illis que similiter qui assumpto vel assumendo crucis signaculo sunt personaliter profecturi.

Nos et fratres nostri sanctae Romanae ecclesiae cardinales plenarie decimam persolvemus sciant que se omnes ad hoc fideliter observandum per excommunicationis sententiam obligatos ita quod illi qui super hoc fraudem scienter commiserint sententiam excommunicationis incurrant.

Sane quia iusto iudicio coelestis imperatoris obsequiis inhaerentes speciali decet praerogativa gaudere crucesignati a collectis vel talliis aliis que gravaminibus sint immunes quorum personas et bona post crucem assumptam sub beati Petri et nostra protectione suscipimus statuentes ut sub archiepiscoporum episcoporum et omnium praelatorum ecclesiae dei defensione consistant propriis nihilominus protectoribus ad hoc specialiter deputandis ita ut donec de ipsorum reditu vel obitu certissime cognoscatur integra maneant et quieta et si quisquam contra praesumpserit per censuras ecclesiasticas compescatur.

Si qui vero proficiscentium illuc ad praestandas usuras iuramento tenentur adstricti creditores eorum ut eis remittant praestitum iuramentum et ab usurarum exactione desistant eadem praecipimus districtione compelli.

Quod si quisquam creditorum eos ad solutionem coegerit usurarum eum ad restitutionem earum simili cogi animadversione mandamus.

Iudaeos vero ad remittendas usuras per saecularem compelli praecipimus potestatem et donec illas remiserint ab universis christifidelibus per excommunicationis sententiam eis omnino communio denegetur.

Iis qui Iudaeis nequeunt solvere debita in praesenti sic principes saeculares utili dilatione provideant quod post iter arreptum quousque de ipsorum reditu vel obitu cognoscatur usurarum incommoda non incurrant compulsis Iudaeis proventus pignorum quos ipsi interim perceperint in sortem expensis deductis necessariis computare cum huiusmodi beneficium non multum videatur habere dispendii quod solutionem sic prorogat quod debitum non absorbet.

Porro ecclesiarum praelati qui in exhibenda iustitia crucesignatis et eorum familiis negligentes exstiterint sciant se graviter puniendos.

The Scriptorium Project is the work of a small group of lay people of various apostolic churches who are interested in the preservation, transmission, and translation of the works of the early and medieval church. Our efforts are to make the works of the church fathers accessible to anyone who might have an interest in Christian antiquities and the theological, philosophical, and moral writings that have become the bedrock of Western Civilization.

To-date, our releases have pulled from the Greek, Syriac, Georgian, Latin, Armenian, Indo-Persian, Germanic, Nordic, Slavic, Celtic, Ethiopian, and Coptic traditions of Christianity, and have been pulled from sundry local traditions and languages.

www.ingramcontent.com/pod-product-compliance
Lightning Source LLC
LaVergne TN
LVHW061041070526
838201LV00073B/5135